THIS BOOK WAS CHOSEN FOR

DATE

CHOSEN

A 30-DAY DEVOTIONAL FOR WOMEN

from Seacoast Sisterhood

Edited by Marney McNall and Sarah Wolf

SEACOAST CHURCH

Chosen

Published in Charleston, South Carolina, by Seacoast Church.

Seacoast Church titles may be purchased in bulk for educational, business, fundraising, or sales promotional use. For information, please email mtpbookstore@seacoast.org. All proceeds help support our global missions initiatives.

Cover art by Emily Reyna
Cover & interior design by Typewriter Creative Co.

ISBN 979-8-9988987-0-9 (Paperback)
ISBN 979-8-9988987-1-6 (Hardcover)
ISBN 979-8-9988987-2-3 (eBook)

To every woman who doubts she is chosen but wants to gain confidence in recognizing God's purpose in her life.

CONTENTS

This devotional reflects the theme from each of the Chosen Women's Conference's fifteen events.

GLORY

LET THERE BE LIGHT

"Tell them they are Chosen."

INTRODUCTION

WHAT DO WOMEN MOST NEED TO HEAR?

In 2011, when Seacoast Sisterhood began dreaming about the possibility of creating a women's conference, this was the central question that needed answered: *What do women most need to hear?* Despite numerous suggestions and brainstorming, nothing resonated—until the day our sisterhood pastor happened to read Isaiah 61.

The Sovereign Lord has filled me with his Spirit. He has chosen me and sent me to bring good news to the poor, to heal the brokenhearted, to announce release to captives and freedom to those in prison. Isaiah 61:1 (GNT)

The answer came back clearly then: "Tell them they are Chosen."

There it was. Chosen. Period. No question mark. It suddenly seemed so obvious. Women needed to know they were chosen by God.

We still do. In ministry, we often see women isolate themselves when hurting. We see how they doubt that God has given much thought to their individual purpose. Yet, from our perspective, it's easy to see that God has so much more for them—for us all—than we let ourselves imagine. For each of us, he has something special in mind, something he has chosen us to be and to do.

Over the years, Chosen has become much more than a conference. It has helped women find renewed purpose, community, and a sense of belonging.

WHO SHOULD READ THIS BOOK?

This 30-day devotional is for women everywhere, who are looking to become more confident in their God-given purpose. No need to have gone to the conference—although, it's great if you have!

WHY READ THIS BOOK?

As a sisterhood, we know the power of sharing our stories, how we can encourage and grow stronger together. That's why this devotional features women's stories and focuses on applying the Word of God to our everyday lives. You will notice this book reflects the theme from each of Chosen's fifteen events and includes two devotions paired with each theme. Told with honesty and vulnerability, each devotion includes a key scripture, devotion, reflection, and prayer of hopeful faith.

This *Chosen Devotional* serves as a reminder that you are significant in God's plans, and that he will equip you to fulfill them.

We hope this devotional will help you:

- Recognize you're not alone.

  Sharing stories helps us connect with each other. It's easy to think no one has gone through what we have—until we hear or read about someone else, who has had a similar experience. Our personal stories are unique, absolutely true, but we hope you'll find some commonality here. Notice how women approach difficult situations differently and rely on their faith to break old patterns and chains, or how they celebrate and find joy in the middle of less-than-perfect circumstances. It may change your perspective.

- Equip yourself with biblical truth to hold onto in tough spots.

  There's likely to come a time when we find ourselves in over our heads. To know the Bible and have God's Word at the ready, to apply it to our lives, will help us beyond measure.

- Discover your worth and a community to encourage you.

  Many of our stories are not meant to be kept to ourselves. When we're bold and vulnerable, we can build each other up with the power of our testimonies; but we must first share them. Find a community where you can get real and hear the stories of others to help you live out your faith.

This *Chosen Devotional* is a celebration of women becoming more confident in recognizing God's purpose in their lives and fearlessly living it out.

Believe it. God sees your worth. After all, he chose you.

While none of the devotions go into detail regarding traumatic situations, some topics may be triggering for some readers. This book contains brief references to anxiety, depression, abuse, sexual assault, addiction, health diagnoses, divorce, and grief. We hope you will note the road to healing that God is walking with each woman, patiently keeping to her pace.

chosen.

...THE LORD YOUR GOD HAS CHOSEN YOU OUT OF ALL THE PEOPLES ON THE FACE OF THE EARTH TO BE HIS PEOPLE, HIS TREASURED POSSESSION.

DEUTERONOMY 7:6 (NIV)

Chosen. The very word speaks to our hearts, doesn't it? We all want to be chosen, don't we? Whether it is being chosen as a friend, a teammate, an employee, or a fiancée, we all long for someone to choose us, to tell us that we are of value. The truth is that we have been chosen, each and every one of us. Before we were even born, God chose to love us, to pursue a relationship with us. He has chosen you, and he wants to use you to help change the world.

Our role in his Kingdom calls us to live in the freedom he offers, and that comes with a sense of purpose and responsibility. As we learn to steward his calling in our lives, we can rely on the confidence and strength he provides. Even when we don't feel worthy of the call, he reminds us that we are significant in his plans, and he equips us to persevere. With the King by our side, we can experience the fullness of joy, peace, and love, and receive his gifts in ways we never imagined.

The Creator chose us. He's our provider, our protector, and our redeemer. Will you accept his invitation to walk boldly with him—loved, empowered, and never alone?

CHOSEN.

The Sovereign Lord has filled me with his Spirit. He has chosen me and sent me to bring good news to the poor, to heal the brokenhearted, to announce release to captives and freedom to those in prison.

Isaiah 61:1 (GNT)

BY DEB HOPPER

The sting of being overlooked or rejected can stay with you for years. When I was a sophomore in high school in the 1970s, I remember being on the prom decorating committee and staying to serve the refreshments. I watched the junior and senior couples enter the gymnasium and took notes as I dreamed about when I could go the following year.

I longed for prom—imagined the dress, the moment, the belonging. But the invitation never came—not as a junior or a senior. In the '70s, you didn't attend prom alone or with your girlfriends. You were either invited by a boy, or you stayed home. The rejection—not being chosen—lingered with me for years. And as an adult, when I walked through the heartache of divorce in my first marriage, I felt rejection on an entirely new level.

During those days of being single again, God became my best friend and partner. He was the first one I spoke to every morning and the last one I spoke to when I laid my head on the pillow at night. The Bible became more than just distant words in an ancient text, I read it as a love letter written to me. I was hungry to understand it and apply it to my life, so I attended Bible studies and conferences to learn more about his Word.

After hearing a message preached on Isaiah 43 at a conference, I opened my Bible to that chapter and read it as a personal message to me from God. Isaiah 43:1 (NIV) spoke the words, "Do not fear, for I have redeemed you; I have summoned you by name; you are mine."

God—the Creator of the universe—called me by name. Not as an afterthought, not out of pity, but because he *chose* me. Isaiah 61:1 (GNT) confirmed it. He has chosen me. I was chosen by God. He called me by my name. It became a marker of belonging like I had never experienced before. A decade later, I was remarried with three daughters and knew they would also need to know this truth. I shared it with them, wanting them to understand how loved they are by God.

And I wanted other women to realize it, too. When we started the Chosen Women's Conference in 2012, my prayer was that every woman who attended would know they were *chosen* by God and would see this truth as a central pillar for their lives. One of my daughters, hearing what we were going to name it, wrote it out in a large script font: CHOSEN and ended it with a period.

Now, it's time for you to put a period at the end of that word. CHOSEN.

God knows our flaws, our past, our struggles—and still he says, "You are mine." To anyone who feels unseen, unloved, or unwanted—you have never been overlooked by God. He has called you, chosen you, and declared that you belong.

> *"The Bible became more than just distant words in an ancient text, I read it as a love letter written to me."*

PRAYER

Lord, silence the lies that tell me I am not enough. Though humans might have rejected me, I have been selected by you. I receive your truth—I am chosen, seen, and loved. Thank you for calling me yours. Amen.

REFLECT

Do you believe that God has chosen you? If not, what are you letting hold you back from becoming who God called you to be?

chosen

A STRETCH FOR ME

We know, dear brothers and sisters, that God loves you and has chosen you to be his own people.

1 Thessalonians 1:4 (NLT)

BY TARA L. BANKS

Have you ever been chosen for something you felt unqualified to do? I'd been the Worship Director for our church for two years when the Chosen Women's Conference team approached me about leading worship at this exciting new event they were planning. I knew it was going to be something special. I was honored and excited to be a part of it.

But then, they asked if I would not only lead worship, but help craft the entire worship experience. That was a little more daunting. My excitement turned into fear and self-doubt. In so many ways, I felt inexperienced for this level of responsibility. While I am used to singing onstage and being involved in creative aspects of ministry, I actually do some of my best work behind spreadsheets and in detailed planning and keeping things organized. So, a conference *experience?* That was going to be a stretch for me.

Did I feel fully qualified for the task? No. Was I confident in all the decisions I would need to make to create a worship experience where a thousand women could authentically and powerfully meet with Jesus? Not at all. But something in me knew that even with my shortcomings, God was in control, and he simply needed me to be willing. So, I agreed.

I knew I'd need to surround myself with incredible creatives and organize the best team of musicians. Together, we'd plan special elements and worship sets that worked with the conference theme. I would coordinate with speakers, hosts, tech and production to make everything feel *seamless*, to eliminate unnecessary distraction, so that the Spirit of God could freely move among the women.

As Paul reminds us in 1 Corinthians 12:12–27, God designed each of us perfectly with specific gifts and although we work individually, we are parts of one body (and together, we truly are better).

After the Chosen Conference was over that year, I was able to look back and see how God had equipped me for a new level of leadership I didn't think possible. I realized he had been preparing me with other, smaller leadership experiences and lessons-learned that "just so happened" to apply to this one. He had been planting seeds for years and knew when it was time for them to bloom.

When someone recognizes a value that you bring to the workplace, event, or moment and asks you to step up and step into a greater role and contribute that part of yourself, I believe the Lord is offering you a chance to really grow. It is that beautiful intersection of the gifts and talents God has given you, and faith in his will for your life. Don't let doubt steal away these opportunities. Trust that God chose you.

> *"He had been planting seeds for years and knew when it was time for them to bloom."*

PRAYER

Father, we thank you that you love us and have chosen us to be your own. We don't have to do everything perfectly, you never ask that of us, but we do put our full trust in you and thank you for your great love that declares we are chosen to be yours. Amen.

REFLECT

What steps have you taken in faith that have shown you how much God loves you and has chosen you to be his own?

chosen

BUT YOU ARE A CHOSEN PEOPLE, A ROYAL PRIESTHOOD, A HOLY NATION, GOD'S SPECIAL POSSESSION, THAT YOU MAY DECLARE THE PRAISES OF HIM WHO CALLED YOU OUT OF DARKNESS INTO HIS WONDERFUL LIGHT.

1 PETER 2:9 (NIV)

If we painted our own portraits, would it reflect how the world sees us—or how God sees us? Would it show who we really are? We often put on different personas to reflect who we think we're supposed to be. We accept flattering labels like "driven, independent, strong, free-spirited" to momentarily boost our sense of worth. In our portraits, would we want to smudge away the harsh labels of our pasts, that stand out as flaws? The portraits we create can so easily obscure our true value.

The truth? Our identity is not found in the world, but in our Father. We are Daughters of the King. God has made each of us in his image. He loves us and has created us for a purpose. We can approach the throne with confidence, as his daughters, and welcome the blessings and promises he has in store. It's time we picked up our crowns.

TRUE IDENTITY

So you are no longer a slave, but God's child;
and since you are his child, God has made you also an heir.

Galatians 4:7 (NIV)

BY MEGAN FERRELL

I went to bed, recounting everything I'd done wrong that day. I let someone down at the bookstore (bad boss); I was too tired to go to an oyster roast with my husband (bad wife). I hadn't spoken to my dad in over a month (bad daughter), and when I finally did call him, I spent most of that time yelling at my kids to be quiet (bad mom). In my head, I heard, "You're a failure."

Have I failed in areas? Yes. Does that make my whole identity a failure? No. I can see now that this was the enemy whispering lies to me. "Are you really a leader? What a terrible wife you are. A good mom would never raise her voice."

Satan is even referred to in the Bible as "The Accuser." We see it firsthand when Jesus was in the wilderness for 40 days and Satan twisted scripture, repeatedly questioning him about his identity.

> Then the devil took him to the holy city and had him stand on the highest point of the temple. "If you are the Son of God," he said, "throw yourself down. For it is written: "'He will command his angels concerning you, and they will lift you up in their hands, so that you will not strike your foot against a stone.'" Jesus answered him, "It is also written: 'Do not put the Lord your God to the test.'" Matthew 4:5-7 (NIV)

Since Satan used this specific tactic to take his shot at Jesus, he must have considered it one of his most convincing. If he used it against Jesus, he'll definitely use it against us. So, we must be aware of his schemes and stay firmly rooted in scripture and in our true identity.

My daughter and I often watch the animated movie "Tangled" and recently, I've noticed the spiritual parallels between us and Rapunzel. For years, she didn't know she was a daughter of the king. She allowed a witch to manipulate and keep her locked in a tower, squashing her power. After discovering her true identity, Rapunzel fights for freedom, returns home to be with her family, and steps into her inheritance as royalty. An heir to the kingdom.

The same is true for us. Without knowing our true identity in Jesus, we are trapped and powerless. But when we follow Jesus, we are adopted into THE royal family, where we can operate in the limitless power and authority of our Father. There is nothing we can do to earn our place in God's family because Jesus did it for us. When God sees us, he sees Jesus, holy and blameless. He wants to give us an incredible inheritance. But first we must accept who we are: Daughters of the King.

> *"When God sees us, he sees Jesus, holy and blameless. He wants to give us an incredible inheritance. But first we must accept who we are: Daughters of the King."*

PRAYER

Father, thank you that we get to call you exactly that, our Father. Help us to walk in freedom and in communion with you as your daughters. Deliver us from the lies of the enemy and help us remain deeply rooted in your truth and your love. Amen.

REFLECT

Who does God say you are? What are some scriptures you can memorize to help you stay rooted in who you are when the accuser tries to lie to you?

chosen

LEMON-WHAT?

Now if we are children, then we are heirs—heirs of God and co-heirs with Christ, if indeed we share in his sufferings in order that we may also share in his glory.

Romans 8:17 (NIV)

BY KATIE WALTERS

I wanted our girls to take ballet, but we couldn't afford it. My husband, Josh, and I had just moved to Charleston, South Carolina for his job in children's ministry, and we were doing our best in our little duplex with three kids, stretching every dollar. I prayed for God to help us give our girls this opportunity and not long afterward, I met a woman in our church who had a ballet studio in her home. In exchange for my two girls taking a class once a week, I offered to babysit her kids.

Every Monday evening, I sat upstairs with her two precious kids and their housekeeper, wiping little faces and helping fold tiny socks. One night, the teacher casually mentioned their family had spent the summer in Italy and how I must try limoncello. I smiled and nodded, but inside, I was thinking: *Lemon-what? I'm just trying to afford gas this week!* It was one of what felt like a million moments since moving to this beautiful but expensive city where I felt completely out of place, like I had stepped into a world that spoke a language I didn't understand.

Then, Josh became a pastor, and suddenly, we weren't just attending church—we were leading! Although the promotion was a good thing, it added pressure. One night after the ballet class, I sat in my old, purple station wagon, wondering how I could lead spiritually when I felt like an outsider.

And right there, I felt God whisper, "You are a daughter of the King."

Honestly? That phrase felt just as foreign as summers in Italy. Daughter? A Father who adores me, who stays and lifts my head? A Father who restores my honor? It taught me that when something in the Kingdom feels unfamiliar, it's not exclusion—it's an invitation. God wasn't pointing out what I lacked; he was inviting me to discover who I truly was.

That moment marked a turning point. I am a daughter of the King. It became a source of confidence. I stepped into leadership opportunities I would have previously avoided. I didn't feel qualified, but I knew I was called. When asked to speak or lead, I reminded myself: *My Father has sent me. I belong here.* It didn't happen overnight, but slowly my posture shifted from hesitant to bold, from self-doubting to secure.

I belong because my Father says I do. And that's far more important than any status, bank account, or background. To this day, when I feel out of sorts, I see it as an invitation to go to my Father, the King and ask, *What do you say about this, Lord?*

I am his daughter, and so are you. We don't have to strive for a place at the table—we already have a seat.

> *"We don't have to strive for a place at the table—we already have a seat."*

PRAYER

Father, remind me today that I am your child. Help me to walk in the confidence of my identity as a daughter of the King. When I feel out of place, unqualified, or unseen, help me to recognize that my inheritance is secure in you. Amen.

REFLECT

Where in your life have you felt like an outsider, and how does knowing you are a daughter of the King change your perspective?

chosen

FOR SUCH a TIME as THIS

...AND WHO KNOWS BUT THAT YOU HAVE COME TO YOUR ROYAL POSITION FOR SUCH A TIME AS THIS?

ESTHER 4:14 (NIV)

A pivotal decision, a leap of faith—stepping into the unknown is a risk that requires courage. We find ourselves facing insurmountable odds and giants of the unseen world. We feel hurled into a battle we know little about. Now is the time of desperation when counting on God is no longer an option—it is a must.

Our understanding cannot contain the scope of the task. We know the enemy will try his most strategic plays, but we can overcome him by the blood of the lamb and the word of our stories.

Do we trust God's purpose in our lives? Esther was not crowned as a queen for her own benefit. She was called to risk her life to save her people. While our decisions may not be life-threatening, we have choices to make—remain silent and do nothing—or step forward and trust our Creator. God positions us to further his kingdom. Will we accept the role he gives us? Will we live boldly in such a time as this?

GRATITUDE CAN REWRITE STORIES

You turned my wailing into dancing;
you removed my sackcloth and clothed me with joy,
that my heart may sing your praises and not be silent.
Lord my God, I will praise you forever.

Psalm 30:11-12 (NIV)

BY STEPHANIE LAMMERS

We were just six weeks away from launching our brand-new church—something my husband and I never dreamed we'd be doing. We weren't "experts" in church planting; we were simply a young family, saying yes to God's stirring in our hearts.

We had spent months praying, preparing, and gathering a small team. We were full of excitement, full of faith...and nerves, too. Yet, we knew God had called us, so we stepped forward in obedience.

Then came the unexpected. My dad—my strong, steady dad—suddenly became sick. What we thought was a simple illness turned out to be a rare infection that spread quickly. I remember curling up in my bed, crying out to God to heal him.

Two weeks later, my dad was in Heaven, and it sent grief washing over me. The girl who once sang about God's goodness, now found herself quietly wondering, "God, are you still good to me?"

It was a tender, fragile season, full of heartache—but it was also a time of major importance to us. In continued obedience, we launched the church, even as the joy of pushing that dream forward was mixed with grief.

Almost a year after my dad passed away, a dear friend who had walked her own road of grief, noticed something I didn't: I was stuck—stuck in the heaviness, stuck in the questions. Gently, she encouraged me to take a brave, small step: spend extended quiet time with God, not just pouring out my heart, but really, really listening.

And it was there, in the stillness, that God so sweetly whispered to my heart. *Fix your eyes on my goodness. Remember my faithfulness. Anchor your heart in who I am. I am your loving, Heavenly Father. Turn your heart to gratitude—because gratitude will break the heaviness off of you.*

And it did.

At first, I noticed one small thing to be thankful for. Then, I noticed five. Gradually, the heaviness began to lift. Gratitude didn't remove my grief, but it reframed it. I began to see the gifts right in front of me: my husband's steady encouragement, the laughter of my three boys and my daughter filling our home, and the faithful, never-leaving presence of a God who was still good, even in my heartbreak.

Gratitude didn't change my story—but it changed me in the story. It opened my eyes to a deeper faith. It gave me greater empathy for others walking through hard stuff and a deeper sense of mission to share the hope and joy of Jesus—to encourage others who might feel stuck.

God had so much more in store for us: more joy, more peace, and more purpose. Maybe today you find yourself standing between heartbreak and hope. I want to gently remind you: God's goodness is not defined by how you feel today. His goodness is anchored in the promises of his Word, and his promises are gifts to us. Start small with gratitude. Let God's love rewrite your story, too.

PRAYER

Father, thank you for meeting us in the hard places, as well as the beautiful moments. We don't always understand your timing, but we know that we can trust your plans. Let gratitude rise, even when it's hard, and fill our hearts with hope and joy. In Jesus' name, amen.

REFLECT

When life takes an unexpected turn and your heart feels heavy with grief or fear, what would it look like to pause, notice the goodness of God in small things, and let gratitude become your act of faith?

chosen

HERE WITH ME

In the day of my trouble I seek the Lord;
in the night my hand is stretched out without wearying;
my soul refuses to be comforted.

Psalm 77:2 (ESV)

BY ADRIENNE HONEYCOMBS

The industrial-sized refrigerator that came with our new house almost ended my life.

I was getting a cold bottle of water, when the refrigerator, unbalanced during renovations, fell forward, trapping me face down on the floor. It pinned my left arm. The pain was so intense, I cried out for help, though my husband, Bear, was 2,000 miles away, working on an oil rig. No one knew I was there, except God.

I'd met only one neighbor. No one was coming. To push away the despair, I talked to myself, my dog, my family. I prayed. *God, please be here with me.* I had always believed in God, but I'd never read the Bible; rather I'd used it as a teenager as a place to stash cigarettes.

Day faded to night, and despair set in. I struggled to breathe. And I was so thirsty. Spying a water bottle near my foot, I stretched out a toe, but the bottle spun away. A surge of anger so strong gripped me that I railed at God for abandoning me. Like in Psalm 77:2, I refused to be comforted, but still I desperately sought his presence, even when he seemed absent.

Later, when the phone rang and rang, I prayed Bear would realize something was wrong. But then, silence. I planned my funeral, my arm no longer feeling sliced by razors, but numb. Toxins were building up in my body. I thought, *I'm going to die here.*

Hours passed, and beautiful neon-red poppies began to spark and dance across my vision, flowers similar to many I'd painted in my studio. I heard the words, "You can let go now, no one is coming." I closed my eyes, but instead of letting go as if abandoned, I gave it all to God, feeling the most beautiful release from the pain and experiencing a peace like nothing I'd ever known.

It was morning, when I heard a knock on the door, and a face appeared in the window. The only neighbor we knew. Bear, sensing something was wrong, had called her. It took four first responders to lift the refrigerator off me. Soon, I was blue-lighted to the hospital.

I eventually lost my lower arm, but I gained so much in a different way. While convalescing, I decided to go to a nearby church—Seacoast—and soon, found myself serving in the children's classroom, much of my time spent drawing for the four-year-olds. The children's reaction to my limb difference varied, some were kind and funny, others scared and unfiltered. It made me wonder how to help normalize such physical differences for children.

When a mother shared, on social media, a sweet photo of her daughter, who has limb difference, it gave me an idea. I asked if I could develop the photo into a painting. That painting led to many others—all highlighting children with disability and difference.

God gave me strength at a time I desperately needed it and led me into relationship with him. He restored me to a place where I could help others. When we surrender to him, he brings us through dark times, such as this, and uses them for purposes unique to each of us.

PRAYER

Dear Heavenly Father, I trust that you are with me, especially in times of anxiety and distress. Please give me the strength so that I can help others find hope and comfort in you, just as I have. In the name of Jesus, amen.

REFLECT

How can you help others find faith and give encouragement when they are facing distress, fear, and doubt?

chosen

chosen
OUT OF THE SHADOWS

WHOEVER DWELLS IN THE SHELTER OF THE MOST HIGH WILL REST IN THE SHADOW OF THE ALMIGHTY. I WILL SAY OF THE LORD, "HE IS MY REFUGE AND MY FORTRESS, MY GOD, IN WHOM I TRUST."

PSALM 91:1-2 (NIV)

We see shadows as dark places where things are hidden, covered up, and maybe forgotten. But in God's shadow, we can find rest. His shadow is a refuge when conflict and uncertainty become too much, when peace feels out of reach.

We declare the Lord as our refuge. Without fail, every hour of every day, his shadow will shelter us. We can trust that he will bring us under his wings and provide a place of comfort, where we are safe, protected, but not in hiding.

When we reemerge, refreshed and refocused, it will be time to go back out into the world. In his presence, he has equipped us with his shield and his strength and with renewed hope to bring others with us to the safe haven of the Almighty.

CLOUDS PARTING

Because of the tender mercy of our God,
whereby the sunrise shall visit us from on high
to give light to those who sit in darkness and in the shadow of death,
to guide our feet into the way of peace.

Luke 1:78-79 (ESV)

BY HEATHER ROSE ARTUSHIN

My best friend, Srijana, and I were midway through our graduate program in social work, when splotches appeared on her skin and her hair began to thin. She was tired all the time. Eventually, she was diagnosed with lupus.

I knew nothing about the autoimmune disease at the time, but Srijana assured me it was treatable. But slowly, my best friend lost weight and didn't look like herself. Not long after landing her first job postgrad, she had to stop working, and eventually couldn't even walk the stairs, her legs swollen and painful.

When she died suddenly, at only 26-years-old, it cast a dark shadow over my life. Grief touched every aspect, especially my work. Yes, I had my own office at a Christian counseling agency, a great supervisor, a good caseload of clients that was building steadily. Yet, every day I crossed the threshold of my sunny office, the darkness of grief came with me. I felt distracted, ineffective. *Why her and not me?* tormented me. I tried to focus on the problems families shared with me. But how could I help them when I felt broken myself?

I thought maybe focusing on building a family of my own might help. When I saw the two pink lines on the pregnancy test, I was elated. Soon, the thought of having a child became all-consuming.

But then, an ultrasound revealed a miscarriage. I needed my best friend, and it was just another cruel reminder that she was gone. I had never felt so alone and empty, desperate to feel God's presence.

I found myself on the other side of the couch, seeing a therapist to process the overwhelming grief of losing my best friend and my child. Healing isn't linear. I'll never be finished grieving Srijana, or missing her presence in my life, or wondering what my child would have been like. But one unremarkable, rainy day, when I came out of a counseling session, I noticed how the clouds had parted and left behind a drippy, quiet calm. I felt the shadows in my life recede just a little. I realized every small effort, every small step mattered.

Every counseling session and prayer helped me accept the losses in my life. But it was a decision I had to make daily. Loss can happen in an instant, but healing takes daily steps of faith in God's direction.

I had a necklace engraved to remember the baby I lost, and I've learned that somehow, past grief can deepen the joy, when it comes. Today, I look at my two sweet boys and am overwhelmed with gratitude to God for his continued goodness. I think about their sweet "Auntie Srijana" and sibling in Heaven. One day, we'll all be together in the happy ending Jesus wrote for our story.

We all find ourselves in the shadows at times. But God has a plan to bring us back out into the light, day by day.

PRAYER

Jesus, fill the dark places in my life with your light, pouring love and grace into my brokenness. Remind me that you are always with me, walking beside me, even through the shadows. Amen.

REFLECT

What shadows are you standing in today? Ask God to pour his light into the darkest places of your life and remind you of his love for you through it all.

chosen

RECOGNIZE THE BLESSING

*This is what the Sovereign Lord says: "Look!
I am going to put breath into you and make you live again!"*

Ezekiel 37:5 (NLT)

BY DANIELLE CABLE

Have you ever felt overwhelmed, even though what was happening was good? When my second baby was born healthy, I was so relieved. Before this pregnancy, I'd had a miscarriage that kept worries and "what ifs" going through my mind. I expected to feel absolute joy now, but as the days passed, I realized how little it took for me to break down in tears. It embarrassed me, made me feel ashamed, and weak. *How can someone with so much joy feel so sad? How can these two emotions coexist?*

Granted, my husband and I had moved into a new home with a new baby, an active toddler, and I had returned to work right after my maternity leave. I was sleep-deprived and most of our family support system was back in Kentucky rather than South Carolina, but that couldn't account for how I was feeling.

After consulting with a couple friends and my doctor, I found myself navigating postpartum depression. And then, my husband suddenly left his job. He had been struggling in a toxic work environment, and it was threatening his sobriety. But we had not discussed or planned for this loss of income! *What just happened, and did he really just say that he had no choice?*

It was too much at once for me. I tried not to be resentful of his decision. Resentment is an emotional beast that will take over your heart and do serious damage to any relationship, draining it of life.

Needing to hear a word from God, I decided to attend my first Chosen Women's Conference. I didn't know many people in our new city yet, and although the thought of going alone terrified me, I reminded myself that I wasn't really ever alone. God was always with me, and that made me brave enough to go.

When one of the speakers talked about God breathing new life into dry bones through Ezekiel's faith, and reviving a vast army, I visualized those dry bones coming back to life...my bones. I sensed that God wanted to help me stop fear and worry from draining the life from my most important relationships. It gave me the hope I needed.

My healing wasn't a sudden miracle. Instead, my relationship with God was stretched and strengthened over time. I went to counseling, spent time with my family, and answered an inner call to become involved in global missions. God used me to minister to other women who were hurting. Sharing how God was healing me, filled my heart with joy.

Although we wouldn't see it for quite some time, the decision my husband made to leave his job ended up being one of the biggest blessings for our family. Although it was a difficult time, it protected his sobriety—now 11 years and counting, which in turn protected our family. If we had not gone through this, we would have missed out on so much in our relationship with God, with each other, and with our children. God has breathed new life into our family, and I've found joy again.

PRAYER

Father, thank you for redeeming me! Please reveal the tender places in my heart that need to be restored. I want more courage to trust you with my circumstances, more faith to praise you in the storm, and more boldness to share my story. In Jesus' name, amen.

REFLECT

In what area of your life have you given up hope? How might you invite Jesus and his redeeming power to come over you?

chosen

FEARLESS

FOR GOD HAS NOT GIVEN US A SPIRIT OF FEAR AND TIMIDITY, BUT OF POWER, LOVE, AND SELF-DISCIPLINE.

2 TIMOTHY 1:7 (NLT)

What scares you? Failure. Rejection. Making wrong choices. You're not enough, you'll let people down. They'll let you down. You should've seen that coming. You missed your chance. Your best days are behind you. Fears whisper in your ears, hoping to take you where you never intended to go and leave you there, alone. Even when you recognize them for what they are, it's impossible to control or escape them on your own.

But there is another voice, clear and perfect calling to you, to us—if we listen and single it out from the rest. This voice will lead us out of the frightening places. God calls us to surrender our fears to him and promises to be with us through anything we face. When he calls, let's turn to him and take his outstretched hand. Follow him past the fears and leave them behind.

God's incredible love and power breaks fear's hold and frees us to boldly step onto the true path he has planned for each of us to follow. Every step toward him teaches us how to become truly fearless.

Day
09

COURAGE IN THE FACE OF FEAR

Be strong and courageous; don't be terrified or afraid of them.
For the Lord your God is the one who will go with you;
he will not leave you or abandon you.

Deuteronomy 31:6 (CSB)

BY HANNAH ERICKSON

"Look, mama! I'm going to do a dangerous stunt!" These exuberant words rang out, and all the mothers at the playground began to anxiously search for this child's mom. "It's me. She's mine," I said, laughing, as I rushed to where my daughter was about to do an acrobatic flip off a high ladder. "I'm coming!" This is normal for Lily. She isn't afraid of much and regularly takes chances in the name of fun and challenging herself.

Even though her "dangerous stunts" can be a source of worry for me as a mother, her courage and zest for life inspires me to be more courageous and fearless in my life. I wasn't like her as a child. I never had the desire to perform any type of "dangerous stunt." I still prefer to calculate my decisions after thinking through all possible outcomes.

As a child, I had test anxiety and feared performing poorly or letting my parents down. In middle school, my family moved to Thailand, which brought out fears of leaving friends and being unable to find new ones who shared my faith. In college, I worried about missing God's "perfect" plan for my life if I didn't make all the "right" decisions.

Looking back, I see how many times I worried in vain. My mom often had to remind me, "Don't doubt in the darkness what you have known to be true in the light." As missionaries, we were accustomed to relying on the Lord, and he always answered our prayers in personal and caring ways, so that we lacked nothing. But still, I tended to worry.

Whenever I'm fearful, I think about when Joshua was to take leadership of Israel. Preparing for the succession, Moses relays God's message and tells Joshua to be strong and courageous, to not be afraid. Later, when it is time to cross the Jordan River into the Promised Land, God, himself, reminds Joshua of this command and reconfirms his commitment to give Israel their long-awaited home. He promises to never leave or abandon them as they walk in obedience to him.

I imagine Joshua still faced fear and uncertainty during the actual battles, but in accepting the challenging circumstances, he led Israel into the Promised Land and into a time of peace. Years later, at the end of his life, Joshua gathered Israel together to recount the history of God's past faithfulness and to remind them to hold fast and not abandon God because he had never abandoned them. This is still true for us today. Whenever fear or anxiousness arises, we can reflect on God's past faithfulness and find strength and courage. If he asks us to do something challenging, he won't leave us to do it alone.

> *"Whenever fear or anxiousness arises, we can reflect on God's past faithfulness and find strength and courage. If he asks us to do something challenging, he won't leave us to do it alone."*

PRAYER

Heavenly Father, thank you for always being faithful to your people and to me personally. Please help me to remember your past faithfulness, when I am overwhelmed with fears. I want to step forward in your confidence and strength. Amen.

REFLECT

How has the Lord been faithful to you in your life? Consider making a list of his past faithfulness for times when you face a new challenge.

chosen

A CALMING BREATH

Do not be anxious about anything, but in every situation,
by prayer and petition, with thanksgiving,
present your requests to God.

Philippians 4:6 (NIV)

BY SUHEY TORRES

The labor and delivery nurse urged me to put my laptop away. It was time to deliver my daughter. The choice to work until that moment was all mine. My anxious nature just didn't let things go unfinished.

This was nothing new. Even as a child, I drove my mom crazy with my incessant worrying and anxiousness. If church started at 9:00am, by 8:30am, I was thinking, *We can't be late. I don't want to walk in late in front of everyone.* Also, I hated the idea of not finishing something and letting others down. I worried about it so much that I started having panic attacks.

My career choice in accounting surprised no one. Numbers are precise and reliable.

When my husband and I were in our twenties, we left everything we knew in Puerto Rico and moved to the continental United States. There, we had to navigate living in a new place that felt foreign to us. Without family nearby, we had the added pressure of doing everything on our own. There was no one else to rely on or take on tasks for us. So, my anxious nature kicked in, telling me I needed to be super-efficient and use my time wisely.

It got to the point where I couldn't fit one more thing into my day and found myself, asking, *How will we make it on our own?* But we weren't meant to carry everything alone. Even with our busy schedules, we needed to make time for God.

In Philippians 4:6 (NIV), God's Word instructs us on how to control our anxious thoughts. "Do not be anxious about anything, but in every situation, by prayer and petition, with thanksgiving, present your requests to God." Our Creator knew we would need help with worry, so he provided the solution in his Word—go to him in prayer.

When I obey his instruction, I see how he guards my heart and mind when things don't go as I plan. Of course, I still have my moments, but I no longer let anxiety paralyze me or dictate how I live my life. In those quiet moments, God reminds me that I'm not carrying the weight of life alone, and he shifts my mind to his blessings.

Today, as a wife and a mom of two children, busy with a full-time career and kids' activities, it's a challenge to keep up. I still worry about failure, but I've learned that God uses my worst days to give me my best days. He is gentle with my cries for help, and he reminds me of his goodness and kindness. He meets me wherever I am, and whenever I need to take a calming breath.

> *"Our Creator knew we would need help with worry, so he provided the solution in his Word—go to him in prayer."*

PRAYER

Father, thank you for guarding my heart and mind in all circumstances, whether I'm overwhelmed with chaos or joy. Help me to pause and breathe as you remove anxiety from my mind. Help me to structure my days according to your plans and not my own. In Jesus' name, amen.

REFLECT

In what areas of your life are you still carrying the weight of life alone, instead of trusting God to protect and provide? How do you see God working when you feel overwhelmed?

chosen

SHINE

THOSE WHO ARE WISE WILL SHINE LIKE THE BRIGHTNESS OF THE HEAVENS, AND THOSE WHO LEAD MANY TO RIGHTEOUSNESS, LIKE THE STARS FOREVER AND EVER.

DANIEL 12:3 (NIV)

Looking up to the heavens, our eyes are drawn to the countless stars that dot the night sky. Even the tiniest glimmer pulls our attention away from the darkness, to where the twinkling stars seem to dance and glow from within.

The night sky that God created can sometimes seem so vast it makes us dizzy. It can make us feel small and insignificant, like one pinprick of light among billions. For centuries, people relied on these individual shining stars to guide them where they needed to go, to help them not get lost. None were insignificant, just as we aren't. He knows us by name. Our Creator wants us to shine like these radiant stars to lead others to him.

When we invite God into our lives, his light fills us like a shining star. His Holy Spirit guides us to do his will and helps us grow in wisdom, learn his Word, and become secure in his love. Like the radiant stars, we are to shine in the darkness and guide others to God—their true home—so they will never be lost again.

LET IT SHINE

Now that I've put you there on a hilltop, on a light stand—shine! Keep open house; be generous with your lives. By opening up to others, you'll prompt people to open up with God, this generous Father in heaven.

Matthew 5:16 (MSG)

BY BLAIRE JOHNSON

It was the last preschool performance of the year. We sat in tight rows of metal folding chairs, holding our printed programs, our phones held high to record the song our children had been rehearsing for weeks. On cue, the children all clicked on their battery-operated candles and sang:

"This little light of mine, I'm going to let it shine..."

This classic children's church song is more than a catchy tune; it's a call to action. So, what does it mean for us to shine our light?

I love the Message translation of Matthew 5:16 that says, "Keep open house." Oftentimes, "open house" makes us think of walking through a house available on the market, or in school, meeting other parents and teachers. But Jesus calls for us to think of our lives as an open house—to make ourselves available for others.

It's not always easy to open up to people and invite them to see the real details of your life. But don't worry about the floors not being swept or the clutter on your counter, because that's what is relatable. By being open, others may see your kindness, your compassion, your hope. One of my high school youth pastors once shared, "You may be the only Bible someone else reads." What he meant was people can learn about Jesus through observation of your life.

Recognize what God has given to you and offer it back to him. He has filled each of us with unique gifts but they're not for us to keep hidden. He wants us to use them to glorify his name. 1 Peter 4:10 (ESV) says, "As each has received a gift, use it to serve one another, as good stewards of God's varied grace."

The "hill" God has placed you on to shine your light could be your neighborhood, workplace, school, family, or even local grocery store! Do not wait to start using the gifts he has given you. And don't believe the lie that someone else can do it better. When we start from a place of surrender, the Holy Spirit can do the rest.

Three months after that preschool performance, our daughter started Kindergarten. I took a walk on the beach to reflect on this milestone and found myself at the Sullivan's Island Lighthouse: a beacon of light to guide sailors to safety, providing direction and hope. It reminded me of Jesus. He is the Light of the World, and we are to reflect that light. So don't hide your light, let it shine bright!

PRAYER

Father, open our hearts to receive the gifts you have given us and open our hands to give them back to you. Allow each of us to be a beacon of light that reflects your love and leads others to know you more. Amen.

REFLECT

How can you choose to shine the light of Christ where God has placed you?

chosen

A FATHER'S LOVE

*You shall also be a crown of glory in the hand of the Lord,
and a royal diadem in the hand of your God.*

Isaiah 62:3 (NKJV)

BY KRISTY GORE

As a child, I was "Daddy's girl." But in 5th grade, while waiting for the morning school bell, my friend mentioned that she'd seen my dad at her neighbor's—a woman who had two daughters. She asked me if I wanted to meet the girls. Confused, I agreed to the introductions, hoping to prove it wasn't him. When I met the girls, I asked a lot of questions.

I realized it was true, and it crushed my heart.

In addition, it placed a burden on me that no child should carry—to tell my mom. I arrived home from school, nauseous at the thought of hurting her. But I did what any 10-year-old would do—I blurted it out—and unknowingly confirmed my mom's suspicions that he was having an affair.

The deep hurt after my dad left me and my mom convinced me that I was unworthy. *Did he love them more than me?* Somehow, I was no longer "Daddy's girl." I wasn't enough.

It changed my view of men and marriage, and as a young adult, I tried to suppress feelings of unworthiness with a promiscuous lifestyle, looking for my value in relationships. For decades, I didn't seek a husband. Marriage seemed nothing more than a signed piece of paper.

Eventually I did get married, but it ended in divorce, causing all the pain from the past to resurface. This experience, however, did push me to seek a relationship with the Lord. Although I had grown up in church, my faith was messy, my view of God mixed with how I saw my earthly father—untrustworthy. When I returned to God and to church, I slowly began to heal and grow.

In 2013, I attended my first Chosen Women's Conference with friends, and to my surprise, the men's ministry was there supporting the event by greeting us as we arrived. A gentleman named Gibson Hopper, dressed in a tuxedo, held out his arm to escort me not only through the front door, but to a full-length mirror. There, he said, "Look at her," and reminded me how much God loved me, which made tears well in my eyes. The reflection staring back at me made me see myself differently—my spirit shining from within made my smile real and radiant for the first time in years.

After two days of having my soul filled during the conference, I left feeling the love of God—knowing my Heavenly Father would never leave me.

Since then, my feelings of self-worth have changed. I have finally found my true value in Jesus. And I am believing that one day, he will bless me with the right man to have as a partner. Until then, I will keep my focus on God because he filled my broken heart and showed me a true Father's love.

> *"The reflection staring back at me made me see myself differently—my spirit shining from within made my smile real and radiant for the first time in years."*

PRAYER

Lord, open my eyes to how much you love your daughter. Show me that I am a royal diadem in your hand. I have worth. I ask that you fill the broken places in my heart and help me see that I am precious and valuable in your eyes. Amen.

REFLECT

What are you allowing to determine your worth and your identity?

chosen

"Recognize what God has given to you and offer it back to him. He has filled each of us with unique gifts but they're not for us to keep hidden."

BLAIRE JOHNSON

be free

MY FRIENDS, YOU WERE CHOSEN TO BE FREE. DON'T USE YOUR FREEDOM AS AN EXCUSE TO DO ANYTHING YOU WANT. USE IT AS AN OPPORTUNITY TO SERVE EACH OTHER WITH LOVE.

GALATIANS 5:13 (CEV)

The sea parted. The Promised Land awaited—the captives were free. There was so much to celebrate! They were about to have a nice and settled, abundant life. But, new commandments, the same daily bread, and wandering in the desert threatened this idea of freedom. Where is this Promised Land?

The road to freedom is rarely straight. Obstacles block our path, and we look back tempted to return to what we've known in the past. We grumble about having to take the long way around. But maybe we need time to learn to trust the one who has set us free.

We all have our own form of rebellion in the desert, our own sin and doubt, but God has given us the incredible gift of eternal freedom. Through his only Son, he set us free. However hard the road ahead is, let's keep our eyes on him and take that next step forward to share the freedom of our faith...of knowing God, with others.

RIGHT WHERE YOU ARE

And you are living stones that God is building into his spiritual temple.

1 Peter 2:5 (NLT)

BY SARAH WOLF

As a new mom, I would carry groceries in one hand, hold my baby in the other, and persuade my three-year-old to follow us down the sidewalk and up two flights of stairs to our apartment. Racing the nap-time clock, I dreamt of the day when I could park in front of an actual house, just steps from the front door.

For years, our downstairs neighbor's complaints about our "loud" footsteps made it hard for our young girls to have friends visit. Without the space to spread out, the apartment became easily cluttered, and it so often consumed my mind that I spent more time cleaning than playing with my kids. I prayed for something to shift, for us to find a home that would fit our family and be affordable. But it was like a boulder was blocking our plans for a permanent home.

One evening, discouraged after another encounter with the neighbor, I came across 1 Peter 2:11 (NLT). "Dear friends, I warn you as 'temporary residents and foreigners' to keep away from worldly desires that wage war against your very souls." Maybe I was the one getting in the way. Maybe I was the boulder—so focused on having a house that I was missing what God had in mind for me at that moment. I certainly wasn't being a "living stone" for God to build on, like Peter described in 2:5. God chose us as believers to become a spiritual temple with Jesus as the cornerstone. He built us into his plans, but I needed to do my part.

To find peace in our situation, I decided to approach things differently and use our temporary living space as a time to become closer to people around me...share meals with neighbors, carpool kids to school, plant in the community garden, and babysit for a mom who lived in our building. I learned that no matter where we are, as believers, we are called to be a part of building God's Kingdom by bringing hope and light to those around us.

For ten years, God strengthened our faith with every signature on the annual lease. He used apartment living to help us trust his plans while we waited on him to provide.

When God blessed us with the right house for our family, we celebrated by jumping up and down on the floor of our second level—a celebration of God's provision, and *maybe* even the joy of not disturbing anyone.

Today, it never gets old pulling into the driveway. I'm grateful for God's faithfulness and his perfect timing. Challenges still arise with home ownership, but God always reminds us of those days in the apartment where he grew our trust in him. When we release our plans to him, we can live in freedom right where we are and be a living stone for God to build on, not a boulder blocking his purposes and his timing.

> *"God chose us as believers to become a spiritual temple with Jesus as the cornerstone. He built us into his plans, but I needed to do my part."*

PRAYER

Father, thank you for trusting me with your building plans and for providing a permanent place in your Kingdom. Help me to see others who need to know you and equip me to care for them. Teach me to trust your plans and to find peace in you and not the things of this world. Amen.

REFLECT

How is God asking you to be a "living stone" for others right where you are?

chosen

CREATE!

That person is like a tree planted by streams of water, which yields its fruit in season and whose leaf does not wither—whatever they do prospers.

Psalm 1:3 (NIV)

BY JENNY MAYER

For years, I have worked on house projects and enjoyed using power tools, but I never thought of myself as having a natural gift toward the arts or creativity. I simply loved taking old, worn-out pieces of furniture headed for the dump and restoring them to something valuable again. Clearing a space in my garage, it was rewarding to sand and paint and use my hands to restore and create new things. And there was not a doubt in my mind that God was using it to help me deal with my breast cancer treatments that had me on a long and uncertain road to healing.

But still, I felt something more welling up inside of me, a longing to: Create! Create! Create! *But create what?* I felt insecure about exploring new creative outlets because I lacked the knowledge and know-how. But how were you supposed to know if you might be good at something if you never tried it? Who said you had to stay in one lane just because that's the one you knew and had come across first? I felt like God was nudging me. *Who said it wasn't your gifting?* I wouldn't know unless I tried. I realized God wanted me to explore what I loved, what brought me joy.

I've learned that creativity comes in many forms. I have always loved springtime and watching God awaken the world from winter's cold and dreary sleep. On my drives to and from work or school drop offs, I started memorizing which plants broke free from dormancy first, which buds swelled on bare branches. After cutting back my crepe myrtles severely in the winter, I saw how it made the leaves, and later flowers, come back stronger than ever. The ability to cultivate growth unlocked something in me, as if my soul bloomed just the same way, even as I continued through difficult treatments. It was life-giving.

I planted a garden and watched tiny seeds break through the soil as seedlings. It was so satisfying to watch them grow, to see I had a hand in creating new life. It was then I heard the Lord. *You know that I look at you as one of those tiny seedlings I planted in good soil. I cannot wait to watch as you flower into a new, wonderful creation. I want the best of the fruit you grow to be used to accomplish my purposes.* It helped me understand how much God, our Gardener, obsesses over us—planting and waiting, watering and fertilizing—so he can see us grow and help others do the same.

In the summer, I picked juicy tomatoes from vines I'd grown from seeds back in February. A gardener is a creator. I realized I was free to create, to "throw off" the insecurities that kept me from exploring what I loved without being an expert. I could become more of the person God created me to be.

> *"It helped me understand how much God, our Gardener, obsesses over us—planting and waiting, watering and fertilizing—so he can see us grow and help others do the same."*

PRAYER

God, thank you for your wonderful creation all around me and within me. Your faithfulness reminds me to be patient with myself as I become who you have made me to be. Thank you for giving me the gift of seeing the fruits of my labor. May they be shared with others to accomplish your purpose for me. Amen.

REFLECT

Has God been nudging you to step out and explore something new? What dormant seeds might be just waiting inside you?

chosen

DANGEROUS

BUT IF IT IS FROM GOD, YOU WILL
NOT BE ABLE TO STOP THEM...

ACTS 5:39 (BSB)

Danger is relative. To a child, a stove can hurt. To a chef, it's an old friend. Water and fire can kill, and yet, they can support life. Sometimes even our faith can be dangerous—if it's trust in the wrong things. For all of history, humanity had gone one way. Then, Christ came, and he taught us to follow him in the opposite direction. When we choose faith in Christ, he will for certain change our lives, but he also calls us to live dangerously.

We may confront our pasts, challenge the status quo, and hold fast to our purpose with single-minded intent. All because he called us to make a difference in a world that loves sameness. Faith in Christ drops us to our knees in humility and at the same time, makes us bold. We may cross into unknown territory, draw lines in the sand, and forgive in the name of freedom instead of fairness.

God did not call us to sit down and be quiet. We are called to fight for what we believe in. No matter how hard the world pulls at us, we do not belong to it. We are his. And we are dangerous.

Day 15

A DANGEROUS "YES"

Then I heard the Lord asking, "Whom should I send as a messenger to this people? Who will go for us?"
I said, "Here I am. Send me."

Isaiah 6:8 (NLT)

BY JENNA SURRATT

One morning, I was reading about Jesus washing his disciples' feet, saying to them, "I have given you an example to follow. Do as I have done to you" (John 13:15 NLT). As I read the words, I felt the Holy Spirit prompt me to go wash the feet of my neighbor's mom. In thinking about Jesus washing the disciples' dirty feet, I greatly appreciate the metaphorical symbolism of this act of service, but it's a whole different story to think about the awkwardness of an actual foot washing.

It felt like obedience wasn't optional, but I had no idea how to make it happen without seeming like a complete wacko. I mean, I barely knew my neighbors. However, they knew my family was involved in church, and a few days prior, they had unexpectedly asked me to come in and pray over their mom because they had gotten news that she didn't have long to live.

But still. Go over and ask to wash her feet? I went about my very full day, and as I was walking in the door that afternoon with my hands full, and kids in tow, my phone rang. It was my neighbor asking if I could come sit with her mom for an hour while she went to pick up meds. Yes! I thanked the Lord for the convenient timing of this request.

When I arrived, my neighbor's mom was non-responsive. I put on worship music, prayed over her, read scripture, and washed her feet with some wipes and rubbed them with lotion. What I thought would be scary was actually incredibly peaceful. In Isaiah, the Lord asks a question I feel he wants us all to answer: "Whom shall I send, and who will go for us?" Isaiah responds, "Here I am! Send me" (Isaiah 6:8 NLT). Oftentimes, a "yes" feels dangerous in the moment, but when our lives are guided by the Holy Spirit, we can trust in his unfailing love and wildly adventurous plans.

I had some experience saying "yes" to God before this: when he brought me to Charleston without knowing a single person in the city; when he sent me on incredible mission trips all over the world; and when he offered me the role of women's pastor, in which I currently serve. None of that would have happened without lots of small "yeses" along the way. Decisions I've made in faith have brought me deeper into intimacy with God and propelled me on my journey with him.

My neighbor's mom ended up going to Heaven, but my "yes" to washing her feet that day opened a door for me to build an unlikely relationship with these neighbors. After many conversations and prayers, they eventually said "yes" to joining us at church! It was there that they experienced the power and presence of God in a palpable way.

The Lord sent me that day on a mission far beyond anything I could see in the moment. We don't always know what is on the other side of our "yes," but that is why it is called walking in faith.

Sometimes, it's a little dangerous, but more important than we could imagine.

PRAYER

Dear God, please give us ears to hear your voice clearly and make our hearts willing and obedient to the leading of your Spirit. Would you fill us with courage to walk into places that feel uncomfortable, but bring us and others closer to you? In Jesus' name, amen

REFLECT

The cross certainly wasn't safe, but Jesus said "yes" to that for you and me. Are you willing to pray the dangerous prayer of "Here I am! Send me"?

chosen

A GOD WHO SEES AND HEARS

Their idols...have mouths, but do not speak; eyes, but do not see. They have ears, but do not hear; noses, but do not smell. They have hands, but do not feel; feet, but do not walk; and they do not make a sound in their throat.

Psalm 115:4–7 (ESV)

BY JACQUAYLE DAILEY

During my quiet time one morning, I decided to have a raw conversation with God. To be honest, I was upset with him. I'd just looked back through my prayer journal and realized I had been praying for the same things as far back as the journal went. Eight years!

I questioned the circumstances going on in my life and why they were happening to me. I was looking for clear direction on where to go with my career—still no direction. I wanted a marriage and a family—and still that had not happened. I was waiting for family reconciliation and peace, and I still had not experienced that. All my adult years so far seemed to have been spent in a waiting room.

When was God going to come get me from the waiting room? When was he going to move in a way that I could see? I wondered if he even heard my prayers.

In my moment of impatience and frustration, God turned my attention to a passage in the Psalms that I had never read that compared God to man-made idols. The comparison struck me so deeply, because our God is all-powerful and all-knowing... and so alive.

Unlike man-made idols, Jesus has a mouth that speaks. He has eyes that see and ears that hear. He has a nose to smell the sweet fragrance of worship and prayer. Our Lord has hands that have touched and healed so many, and feet that have walked this earth. The realization came to me that I had started to create idols in my own life.

Maybe I was holding back, still trusting in the world to make things happen for me rather than Jesus. I was using this world as the measurement of my success and happiness. It felt dangerous to surrender my hopes and dreams, but I needed a reminder that I was talking to the Living God.

When we create idols in our lives, we unknowingly forget about the real and active power of God. The God I serve understands what I am feeling. When we're upset, it can feel dangerous to be honest with him, but he wants that honest, genuine relationship with us.

That day, my reality didn't change, and it still hasn't. But what did change was my perspective about God. I set my eyes back on the Living God. He knows my hopes and what is in my heart. I will put my trust in him. Now, I am focusing on my relationship with him, even as I sit in the waiting room. God knows I am there, and he hasn't forgotten me.

> *"It felt dangerous to surrender my hopes and dreams, but I needed a reminder that I was talking to the Living God."*

PRAYER

God, there is no one like you! Thank you for seeing and hearing us in the most difficult and frustrating times of our lives. God, help us to remember who we are really talking to. Let us never forget how wonderful it is to be known by you. In Jesus' name, amen.

REFLECT

Have you been in the waiting rooms of life? How can you change your perspective on waiting for God to move and restore?

chosen

VICTORY

YOU SEE, EVERY CHILD OF GOD OVERCOMES THE WORLD, FOR OUR FAITH IS THE VICTORIOUS POWER THAT TRIUMPHS OVER THE WORLD. SO WHO ARE THE WORLD CONQUERORS, DEFEATING ITS POWER? THOSE WHO BELIEVE THAT JESUS IS THE SON OF GOD.

1 JOHN 5:4-5 (TPT)

One morning, in the middle of a long war, he emerged from the tomb and the decisive blow was struck. The enemy was defeated.

But our own battles aren't over. We are attacked from all sides, living in a world that tries to make us feel too insignificant to make a difference. But God, himself, fights at our side and he calls us conquerors. We march on with determination because we know he is with us, and we have everything we need to win this fight.

It will take courage to stand up for what is right, but our faith in the One who conquered death gives us hope as we face each battle. We know the truth, and we draw strength from his power and find his peace in the midst of war. We are resilient and will endure. We stand together as a unified body of sisters to tell the world who God is.

The outcome is certain, he has won, the end is in sight, and we press on toward it. We won't wait to celebrate what God has done for us—it's time to sing and shout, Victory!

BACK-TO-BACK

A person standing alone can be attacked and defeated,
but two can stand back-to-back and conquer.

Ecclesiastes 4:12 (NLT)

BY DANI BYHAM

You've seen it in the movies—when two action heroes are surrounded by multiple enemies, and it looks like they've lost the fight. Instead of surrendering, they turn back-to-back, strengthen the grip on their weapons, and re-set. This defensive strategy is sometimes referred to as "mutual support." It helps the underdogs protect their blind spots and can often lead them to victory.

We may never use this fighting technique, but life has a way of bringing all sorts of battles that require a similar strategy. Five years ago, I found out how important it was to enlist the help of a friend during a really tough time. It wasn't like the movies though. It was less choreographed and harder to identify the enemy.

After months of unexplained pain and unhelpful test results, my doctor's final diagnosis was "anxiety." The heart-racing, difficulty sleeping, muscle pains, shortness of breath, tingling in my fingers, and headaches narrowed down to one word. I was skeptical that this was the answer to my physical symptoms, but I was also desperate to feel better. With a bottle of pills and tearful acceptance, I started a year and a half of numbness.

The absence of pain was a welcome relief, but I still wanted to know how I had gotten here. Why had my body rebelled against me? The previous ailments disappeared, but new side effects took their place. My emotions were flat. Brainstorming anything was like trying to march in mud. I lost the desire to read, write, or make art. *Would I feel anything again? Had I lost my creative spark forever?*

I decided to attack the threats to my health on multiple fronts: physical, mental, emotional, and spiritual. If one area was in a deficit, I tried to compensate in others. I took walks, I went to counseling, and I worshipped the Lord. I took a good hard look at what was going on around me and how I was handling it. Medication was a small part of my healing. I was able to wean myself off them in about a year and a half, while taking ground in other areas.

Still, I experienced a season of doors closing, dreams dying, and friendships ending. Sadness and stress wore down my body's defenses without me realizing it, and I felt like I was fighting alone.

But then, a new friend joined my battle. She had just walked through similar struggles and knew a battle strategy. With our backs together, she called out next moves, and I trusted her. Together, we memorized scriptures to combat insecurity and fear. She prayed out loud for me and with me. My friend helped me to recognize specific enemies to my mental and physical well-being.

While the doctors and counselors revealed some of the enemies to my health, most importantly I credit God and this sister for my personal victory, giving me the strength to keep fighting.

> *"With our backs together, she called out next moves, and I trusted her."*

PRAYER

Dear Jesus, thank you for the fellow soldiers you send to make us stronger in the battles that we face. Please show us blind spots that would prevent us from living victoriously. Amen.

REFLECT

Have you been fighting a battle alone? What victory are you praying for?

chosen

VICTORY IS BELIEF

No, in all these things we are more than victorious through Him who loved us.

Romans 8:37 (HCSB)

BY ELIZABETH PATRICK

Little girls are supposed to be loved and protected. But I know what it's like when that doesn't happen. Since the age of seven, I've carried a jagged scar of unworthiness, feeling damaged from childhood trauma and family dysfunction.

Even as an adult, a part of me felt stuck emotionally at seven years old, the wound still open. I wanted to fix the broken part of my soul that told me I was nothing, but my past kept reappearing like a schoolyard bully. Since no one was going to protect me, I had to protect myself. I told myself not to open my heart, not to let others in. Don't trust anyone—especially men with authority. I remained a young girl in a woman's body, desperate to earn the right to be seen, chosen, loved.

I should be a grim statistic. But I'm not. Why? Because one day in my early twenties after a night of drunken partying, a friend looked at me and said: "Do you want to go to church with me?" And for reasons then unknown to me, I said, "Yes." We went to Sunday school, and I sat next to a young man who would introduce me to Jesus—and later become my husband.

His love and support were godsends, but I would still occasionally wear my seven-year-old self, striving for something that couldn't be earned. I thought if I worked harder, had more counseling, read more scripture and declared more verses over my daily life, then I would be victorious. But I wasn't. Because I was fighting with my own strength.

Do you know what I really needed and finally found? Belief—true belief in a God who always loved, valued, and found me worthy. I realized that nothing anyone else did to me, or would do to me, could ever change that love.

It has taken time to fill in those deep ruts of false belief, but I have chosen to believe what God says, over what my experience taught me. I've found victory in trusting that the power our past has over us—the power of God is infinitely MORE!

The fact that I'm still alive, in a healthy stable marriage of 34 years, have three incredible children, love Jesus, and hold places of leadership in my community is only because of God! He mended the wounded parts of my soul. He set me free and gave me victory.

PRAYER

Lord, we strive so hard to be worthy and acceptable. But we already have your approval. You've given us the gift of your love. Help us believe that what you say about us is true and cannot change. Thank you for creating us with inerrant value. Amen.

REFLECT

Is there a wounded "seven-year-old" part of you striving to earn value and worth? How might you be fighting in your own strength?

chosen

"He set me free and gave me victory."

ELIZABETH PATRICK

revel

CELEBRATE GOD ALL DAY, EVERY DAY. I MEAN, REVEL IN HIM! MAKE IT AS CLEAR AS YOU CAN TO ALL YOU MEET THAT YOU'RE ON THEIR SIDE, WORKING WITH THEM AND NOT AGAINST THEM. HELP THEM SEE THAT THE MASTER IS ABOUT TO ARRIVE. HE COULD SHOW UP ANY MINUTE!

PHILIPPIANS 4:4–5 (MSG)

The Law that God gave his people in the Old Testament was full of sacrifices, rules, and consequences, but God also loved a good celebration. We don't often associate God with parties, but we should! One of the most important sets of instructions God gave his people was to feast and rejoice to mark key events that revealed his hand in this world.

Reveling matters to God. Let's not get so caught up in our own troubles that we forget to pause and see all that God has done. Let's not be so quick to already be looking for the next best thing. Take a breath. Smile. Meet up with some friends. Stop and throw a party for taking even a small step in the right direction, toward healing and Jesus.

God wants us to find joy in any circumstance. Take time to revel—to remember God's love and blessings, his provision and protection, his incredible faithfulness. We have so much to be thankful for. It's worth celebrating.

THINGS YOU LEARN WHEN YOU STOP COLORING YOUR HAIR

Gray hair is a crown of glory; it is gained by living a godly life.

Proverbs 16:31 (NLT)

BY NICOLE SEITZ

I made a bold decision several years ago to stop coloring my hair. It was a personal revolution in my eyes, seeing as the women in my family resist aging at every turn. My last coloring was for a high school reunion. But just a month later, something tugged at me—the Lord and my authentic self.

In my twenties, I watched my Aunt Bonnie die of breast cancer at 46. I just wanted to make it past that dreaded age and not share in her fate. So, turning 47 was a moment of liberty. To celebrate, I decided not to cover the gray anymore. Bonnie never got to go gray. I would wear mine proudly.

The problems, though, were many. In my transition phase, I looked untended. I watched as people's eyes went straight up to the shock of gray. Day after day, I had to face other people's glances. I felt like a rebel. Some days I felt like a fool. It was an internal battle waged each day in the mirror. I decided my hair was not gray, but silver. I was growing silver threads and felt blessed by God to see them. I began to feel my decision to stop coloring wasn't just a decision, it was a call.

And in loving mercy, the Lord allowed me to see why he had been calling me there.

One year after I stopped coloring my hair, a month before my 48th birthday, I was told I had breast cancer. Mammograms, biopsies, MRIs, and waiting for results. Coming to terms with my mortality, with the "dadgum it, I did follow in her steps after all" feelings, and finally the acceptance that this was my new mountain to climb. Having cancer is certainly a struggle for your life, but also a struggle for identity. Praise God, he had been slowly dismantling my false identity.

I am not my hair color. I am not my youth. I am not my looks nor femininity. I am his.

Today, I am more authentically me, more authentically his, than I was just over six years ago—silver hair, scars and all. It's been five years since my cancer diagnosis, praise God. Cancer never defined me. God does. He says I am beautiful and of value to him just the way I am. And I can't wait to go all silver because every new strand means another glorious day of living, another thread in my "crown of glory."

> *"He says I am beautiful and of value to him just the way I am."*

PRAYER

Father, thank you for each day that you give me. Help me to see myself in your eyes alone. May my identity be found only in Christ Jesus, as a child of God, fearfully and wonderfully made. Amen.

REFLECT

Do you view getting older as a blessing or a battle? How does your family's and society's acceptance or nonacceptance of gray hair affect your identity as a woman and a child of God?

chosen

DID JESUS LAUGH?

For everything there is a season...A time to cry and a time to laugh. A time to grieve and a time to dance.

Ecclesiastes 3:1, 4 (NLT)

BY JESSICA FACKLER

I have been blessed with a very distinct laugh. Old friends who worked with me at various hospitals, say they still talk about my loud and proud cackle. My coworkers could always find me by following the sound of hyenas.

As a former cardiac cath lab technologist, I made it my life's work to make people laugh on their worst days. Not that there is anything funny about having a heart attack, but asking a patient with chest pain to remove their pants takes finesse! Especially when they'd been told it was just going to be a small stick in the arm.

There is a lot to be said for laughter and its amazing ability to reduce anxiety. In those awkward and dire moments, I needed my patients to feel relaxed (at least a little) and know with confidence that our medical team would do everything we could to save their lives. It was, at times, difficult to ease the tension, but I found that humor always helped. A quick joke or friendly jab always seemed to de-escalate unsteady emotions.

Because laughter is so vital to us, I've often wondered if Jesus ever laughed. There isn't a single verse in the Bible to say he did. It says he wept when Lazarus died; it says he got angry at some merchants and flipped tables, but nowhere does it mention him laughing. Why is that? I understand the role of living Savior is quite serious. Carrying the sin load of all humanity is just not funny. But surely, he laughed at some point. I mean, just look at his 12 chosen friends. There is plenty of comedy to be found in that group. If he wasn't laughing, he would surely have been crying!

Laughter is a reflex. How else would babies know how to smile? It might be because of gas bubbles, but it's still a smile. Laughter is an innate response to joy. Scripture tells us that joy is a gift of the Holy Spirit (Galatians 5:22 NLT). The Bible also tells us to "Celebrate God all day, every day. I mean, revel in him!" (Philippians 4:4 MSG). Laughter is the perfect way to revel in the joy given to us by our Creator.

So, did Jesus ever laugh? I absolutely believe he did. We know Jesus experienced everything humans do: pain, sadness, love, and joy. If we are truly created in his image—quirky laughs and all—then we can be sure he delights in all of his creation. "For the Lord takes delight in his people; he crowns the humble with victory" (Psalm 149:4 NIV). Who knows, maybe Jesus sounded like a hyena, too?

PRAYER

Father, thank you for the gift of laughter. Thank you for the ability to experience joy despite this fallen world. With joy comes hope. And gleefully, our hope is found in you. Amen.

REFLECT

As we go through our day, how can we better share the joy of the Lord? Do those around us see the hope we have in God through our actions...and yes, our laughter?

"If we are truly created in his image—quirky laughs and all—then we can be sure he delights in all of his creation."

JESSICA FACKLER

STRONGER

SHE IS CLOTHED WITH STRENGTH
AND DIGNITY; SHE CAN LAUGH
AT THE DAYS TO COME.

PROVERBS 31:25 (NIV)

What makes a person strong? The world would have us believe that to be truly strong means to be tough, to stand on our own, and not need anyone else. But it's not our physical abilities or our own resilience. Over and over, God likes to take our assumptions and turn them on their heads. It's relying on ourselves that actually makes us weak.

God offers us the most incredible gift: *his* own power, *his* own strength to use to stand firm in our faith and to protect those we love. That's what he offers...if we'll just place our hand in his.

Trusting he is with us, we can prepare for the challenges ahead. When we set our fighting stance, we may discover that we are no longer the same. Something has changed in us. There is a new fire in our souls and steel in our spines. No matter what comes our way, we can throw our heads back and laugh because through him, we are STRONGER.

Day
21

A MIRACULOUS FLIGHT

Have I not commanded you? Be strong and courageous.
Do not be afraid; do not be discouraged, for the Lord
your God will be with you wherever you go.

Joshua 1:9 (NIV)

BY DEBBY DEROSA

I almost didn't try to get onto the flight that would change my faith in miracles.

A Nor'easter was moving along the coast, and I was scheduled to depart from Greenville, South Carolina, for a mission trip to Togo, West Africa. As the only person going from my area, I was to meet up with the team at Newark airport to travel together the rest of the journey.

At 11:00am, my trip leader called. My flight from Greenville had been canceled due to the storm. Could I try to get a flight to Atlanta? If so, I could still connect with the group in Newark. This new flight was departing much earlier, and I was still at work. My luggage was at home, 15 minutes in the wrong direction, and I still needed to add some last-minute items.

As I rushed home, the travel agent called to say he couldn't get me on the flight, but maybe I could go to the airport to ask in person. Chances weren't good, though, because the flight was with a different airline. If that didn't work, I would have to fly out two days later and make the long trip to Africa by myself.

I felt heartbroken. *Should I even go?* This was my first mission trip. I had prayed about it, planned for it, and fundraised for nearly a year. *Was I wrong about God calling me to this?*

I didn't like the idea of traveling to Africa alone, but I didn't want to quit when I was so close. I spoke with my husband, and he thought I should try to get on the flight to Atlanta. So, I drove to the airport, praying, "God, if you really want me to go on this trip, you'll have to get me there."

At the counter, I gave the airline employee my name, and they said I already had a seat on the new flight! Wow. Okay, great! I arrived at the gate during final call. When I sank into my seat on the airplane, I was in silent awe. Through all the chaos, God had made a way. It was a miracle. I started to cry. *How could he care that much for me?*

Meanwhile, the travel agent was telling my trip leader that he couldn't get me on the Atlanta flight. She replied, "She just texted me that she's on the plane. You need to book her connection!"

God had clearly intervened, and I thought that meant I'd do something huge in Togo. But honestly, I played more of a support role on my team. I helped check people in to the medical clinic, played with children, and passed out supplies.

The truth? It was wonderful, but anyone on the team could have done what I did. But the fact God got me there had a serious impact on me personally, showing me that God sees me and cares—that he does intervene.

The miracle's greatest impact was the gift of strengthened faith it gave me. Now, I pray with that belief. God doesn't answer every time in the way I hope, but enough that I keep praying, as a child who truly trusts her Father.

PRAYER

Dear Lord, I believe in your sovereignty and provision. I know you care about even the smallest details of my life. When I get discouraged, help me be strong and courageous to do your will. In Jesus' name, amen.

REFLECT

How has God shown up in an impossible situation for you, and how did it affect your outlook on what he will do in the future?

chosen

STRENGTH IN WEAKNESS

"...My grace is sufficient for you, for my power is made perfect in weakness." Therefore, I will boast all the more gladly about my weaknesses, so that Christ's power may rest on me.

2 Corinthians 12:9 (NIV)

BY HANNAH LAFALCE

When I think of the word "strong," I think of the character, Luisa, from the movie, *Encanto.* My four-year-old used to watch this movie on repeat, and I connected with Luisa's catchy song in a way I did not expect—I noticed a little of myself in her. No, I don't have superhuman strength—I can barely do a push-up—but I often find myself trying to do things in my own strength and that never ends well.

We aren't meant to carry it all. In the movie, Luisa's physical strength makes her useful to her family and the people of her village, but underneath the surface, she fears what everyone will think of her if she can't live up to their expectations. She sings about pressure that never stops. Have you ever felt that pressure?

The pressure to be strong is real—not just physically, but also mentally and emotionally. A quick scroll on social media reveals countless posts on self-help, mindfulness, and various workouts. (I mean, have you seen those crazy tongue exercises?) It's not that all of them are bad, but what if true strength is found in realizing our weaknesses?

After our first child, I quickly realized I could not be a mom in my own strength. I placed so many expectations on myself to have it all together—homemade meals every night, laundry folded and put away, a spotless house, and weeds in the flower bed managed (as if caring for a tiny human was not enough). I tried to check all the boxes and keep up with my never-ending to-do list, but I was frustrated and tired. The key word is *my* to-do list, not God's. I had to come to a place of surrender and recognize my weakness. When I laid down those unhealthy expectations, it allowed me to experience the joy of the Lord, who is my strength.

Apart from God, we can do nothing. His power is made perfect in our weakness. I needed God's help every single day, and I found strength by asking him and others for help. Strength came in knowing when to rest and accepting that some things had to wait. Now, as my children are growing, I need God's strength even more—especially to hold my tongue and be slow to speak. (Toddlers and preteens, anyone!?)

Our worth is not found in our physical or mental strength, or in what we accomplish, but in whose we are. We have something Luisa didn't have—Jesus! He extends a beautiful invitation in Matthew 11:28,30 (NIV), "Come to me, all you who are weary and burdened, and I will give you rest... For my yoke is easy and my burden is light." When we are yoked with Jesus, we can do far more than what's possible in our own strength.

> *"When we are yoked with Jesus, we can do far more than what's possible in our own strength."*

PRAYER

Lord, thank you that your grace is sufficient, and your strength is made perfect in my weakness. Forgive me when I try to carry things on my own. Teach me to rest in your presence, to ask for help, and to find joy in the freedom that comes from relying on you. Amen.

REFLECT

Make a list of the things you try to accomplish in your own strength. How can you begin surrendering each of them to Jesus?

chosen

DEEPER

HE REVEALS DEEP AND MYSTERIOUS THINGS AND KNOWS WHAT LIES HIDDEN IN DARKNESS, THOUGH HE IS SURROUNDED BY LIGHT.

DANIEL 2:22 (NLT)

The surface seems safe and calm, a place known and comfortable. It's tempting to skim our hands over the water and enjoy what's light and carefree and won't weigh us down. But our hearts crave something more, some deeper connection with God and with others. If we wade into the shallows, we begin to see there is so much more below the surface if we are courageous enough to go deeper.

God is calling us there. Into the deep. We do not know what we will find, but we can go there together. More courageous now, we dive in and go where he calls, into cooler, darker waters to where the difficult things we have avoided are waiting for us to set them free. We will not be afraid because God is with us. When we release our fears together, our lungs near to bursting, his presence surrounds us and lifts us back to the light to breathe in a strengthened faith. Together, we are changed.

DIG DEEP

The Lord will surely comfort Zion and will look with compassion on all her ruins; he will make her deserts like Eden, her wastelands like the garden of the Lord.

Isaiah 51:3 (NIV)

BY AMANDA NISWANDER

How do you surrender the wounds you never wanted to acknowledge or reveal? How do you move past trauma without ever verbalizing what happened to you? When a family member called to admit and apologize for the role he played in my childhood abuse, everything in me wanted to deny and shove it back into the deep recesses of my mind and heart where it had resided for over 25 years.

My family member desired freedom from this secret, a clear conscience, but it left me to deal with this admission. The darkness had been limiting the depth of my relationships for all those years. God knew I desperately craved freedom and was exhausted from attempting to reach it on my own. So, I had a choice to make: Keep wrestling with my shame and being a slave to my wounds or dig into my painful memories with the hope that God would heal my heart.

I chose the latter, although it terrified me. I felt the Holy Spirit whispering that what was meant for evil, God meant for good. I chose to use this person's unexpected admission to propel me closer to the source of healing—to the Lord. He gave me an image of myself tending a garden that had become overgrown with weeds. Some weeds budded flowers that almost looked like desired blossoms, others had hidden thorns, and some had deep roots that were seemingly impossible to pull up—deep-rooted lies that I had believed that said I was worthless and pointed to my trauma as proof.

At times, I worried only weeds would ever grow in this garden. But I kept going, digging deeper to clear the way for new life with the help of therapy, a supportive community, and the Lord's gentleness. Finally, I have started to see the garden blossom again with flowers and colors I love that remind me of bright pink petunias and vibrant yellow zinnias.

When we acknowledge the pain in our lives and allow ourselves to dig into where it originated, we create space for growth. Isaiah 51:3 (NIV) says "...he will make her deserts like Eden, her wastelands like the garden of the Lord." God promises to help pull all those weeds with you and speak truth over you in contrast to the lies buried deep in your heart. You do not have to do this alone anymore. Clear out the weeds and create space to plant something new...something beautiful.

PRAYER

Lord, thank you for guiding me through my pain. Your hand has never left me. You lifted me from the darkness of my past and replaced it with the vibrant colors of your glory. I place my shame at your feet and ask that you help me to continue to seek your truth as you plant something new and beautiful in my life. Amen.

REFLECT

Ask God to give you the courage to dig deeper into whatever is preventing you from truly healing. Find a trusted friend, a mentor, or a licensed therapist and share your story.

chosen

INTO THE DEEPEST DARK

When you go through deep waters, I will be with you. When you go through rivers of difficulty, you will not drown. When you walk through the fire of oppression, you will not be burned up; the flames will not consume you.

Isaiah 43:2 (NLT)

BY ELIZABETH REPPARD

There's something about the quiet of the night that causes reflection. The business of the day is done, but in the stillness of the dark, our minds have the space to think, reflect, and recall—whether we want to, or not.

When I was a much younger version of myself in every way, I found myself awake in the middle of the night, crying, having just suffered a painful break-up. I had been accused of something that wasn't true and rejected by someone I truly loved. It had blindsided me. The situation was so unfair that my mind repeatedly and fruitlessly went over how things could have turned out the way they had.

I cried out, looking for solace from the one who created me, and I distinctly remember how the realization hit me that Jesus had been rejected, how he had been betrayed. He knew exactly what I was feeling. I understood his love and sensed his presence, his nearness like never before. It was a defining moment for me, to understand that I had heard from Heaven when I really needed to.

Years later and newly married, I found myself in one of the darkest places of my life. At the altar, I'd had a beautiful picture in my mind of our relationship, but within months, it darkened before my eyes, when I discovered some very destructive patterns in my husband. It shattered me.

Night after night, I would lie awake next to my husband, yet I found myself feeling alone, heartbroken, and utterly rejected, devastated by choices I didn't make, but was left to deal with the consequences.

One night, the darkness felt so impenetrable, I sank into my grief and cried out to God. "Why? Where are you? What are you doing?" It was then I heard in my spirit, words from Heaven go straight to my heart. *You are mine. When you pass through the waters, I will be with you.* I didn't know where they were in scripture. I just knew those words were his. In the morning, I set out to find them.

I found them in Isaiah 43. I felt the love of my Savior minister to my soul, his voice once again finding me in my deepest darkness. While there was no promise to remove all pains and trials; I grasped onto the much-needed reminder that he was with me and always would be.

Many of us avoid the darkest and deepest places inside us because that's where we hide our pain. But God sees all, knows all, and is ever willing to be with us through our pain if we allow it. If you find yourself awake in the quietness of night, trust that God will never leave you, nor forsake you.

> *"I felt the love of my Savior minister to my soul, his voice once again finding me in my deepest darkness."*

PRAYER

Father, no matter what circumstances we find ourselves in, help us to accept your invitation to yield and allow you into our deepest hurts and darkness, so that we can experience the light of life. Amen.

REFLECT

Where do you see God working in your deepest pain? How has he rescued you in the dark?

chosen

"When we acknowledge the pain in our lives and allow ourselves to dig into where it originated, we create space for growth."

AMANDA NISWANDER

Eden

BUT I AM LIKE A FLOURISHING OLIVE TREE IN THE HOUSE OF GOD; I TRUST IN GOD'S FAITHFUL LOVE FOREVER AND EVER.

PSALM 52:8 (CSB)

Eden was our paradise—a place of peace...and beauty...of innocence. Our task was to care for and nurture God's garden, and our privilege was to walk alongside him. He gave us every plant, every seed, every tree—except one.

The whispers of rebellion called, the temptation proved too strong, and we ate of that tree. Expelled from our sacred place of safety, we looked back to find the way shut, barred by flaming sword. Our paradise lost and our story forever altered. But God never left us alone in that in-between land. He sent his Son to overcome death's permanence, its separation, and heal what Adam and Eve had done when they "took and ate."

One day, Jesus will return, and dry deserts will become gardens of lush green again. He will renew humanity, transforming us into the full versions of the people we were meant to be. He will make all things new—a new Heaven and a new Earth. Until that time, we will tend the land we've been given and fulfill his purposes within us. If we pause and listen to the wind through the trees as it touches each leaf it passes, we might hear echoes of it still, echoes of Eden.

NO PLACE LIKE HOME

*Do not repay evil with evil or insult with insult.
On the contrary, repay evil with blessing, because to this
you were called so that you may inherit a blessing.*

1 Peter 3:9 (NIV)

BY VALARIE JONES

We can inherit many things from our families. For me that includes resilience and a love of home, even when that home is far from perfect. My parents, the same as their parents, started off working in fields for farm owners at very early ages. As young adults living in South Carolina, during the early 1900s, they bought their own property and continued farming and selling vegetables in the Charleston City Market. Neither of them completed third grade, but my mother always said she had God's wisdom to guide her.

Along with my nine brothers and sisters, I grew up in church and at the age of twelve accepted Jesus Christ as my Savior. I soon realized that outside of our James Island community, the social atmosphere was a lot worse than I imagined. Being an African American at a white majority college in 1973 caused me to learn what 1 Peter 3:9 was talking about, not repaying insult with insult. I left college after a year and enlisted in the United States Army.

There is no place like Charleston though. I returned after serving for two years, missing my family and the Lowcountry's rich history of black culture, great flower gardens (especially Magnolia), and beautiful beaches. I inherited my mother's business: Virginia's Vegetable Stand, and with each year that went by, I continued to keep 1 Peter 3:9 at the forefront of my mind.

The social atmosphere became better, but not as good as it is today. I remember my mother praying for people who mistreated her because they felt she was less than they were, that she didn't have the education they possessed. She would tell me, "kill them with kindness."

Repaying evil with blessing is engraved in my family heritage, and prayer was the basis of our family's faith and walk with God. God was always at the head of whatever my parents planned or wanted for us. My mother was a true missionary, giving her unsold goods to families in need or sending over a home-cooked dinner.

My parents taught all ten of us, it is better to give than to receive because God will give you what he has for you. Being a native Charlestonian, I have seen so many changes in my lifetime. Charlestonians (all races) used to have separate schools and churches; they didn't live or even travel through certain neighborhoods. Yet now, they live next to each other, learn in the same classrooms, and worship God together. I never understood why it was like that before, but I am so glad it is not like that now.

My mother used to also tell us "Just live." Each day, I try to do that. I see God's blessing and changes in Charleston for the better. But we still have a ways to go. One day, God will transform and redeem the entire world—all the places we love most.

> *"You have provided a way for us to live in unity by sending your Son, Jesus."*

PRAYER

Father, thank you for the gift of family, who pass down your Word and serve as an example of your goodness. You have provided a way for us to live in unity by sending your Son, Jesus. Please help us to see people of different backgrounds, races, and circumstances as your children. I ask that you transform and redeem the world, drawing us closer to you and to each other. Amen.

REFLECT

In what ways can you repay evil and insults with blessings?

chosen

THE LABYRINTH

Stand at the crossroads and look; ask for the ancient paths, ask where the good way is, and walk in it, and you will find rest for your souls.

Jeremiah 6:16 (NIV)

BY MARNEY MCNALL

A rush of anxiety swept through me, though nothing stressful was happening. I couldn't have been more relaxed in an Adirondack chair, chatting with two close friends under some trees on the university green in Newport, Rhode Island. We'd finished grad school together, the previous year, and were visiting as alums. There was no pressure. Still, that flare of anxiety hit, followed by a burst of heat across my neck and chest.

I was familiar with the medication's side effects by now. Not fun, but a better option than the cancer returning. Since movement helped manage the effects, I decided to walk around the green, when my attention caught on the spiral of steppingstones the university called "the Labyrinth."

I'd never taken the time to check it out. I'd read somewhere that labyrinths represented a path going inward, like on a pilgrimage of spiritual transformation. Some medieval churches, like Chartres Cathedral in France, had labyrinths built into their floors. Walking one was meant to help you progressively open your heart to God, as you approached the center.

This labyrinth was a sort-of spiral around 30 ft. in diameter, and at its center was an engraved stone. What was on it? Curious, I started along the labyrinth's path, hoping it would calm me.

When the doctor had told me I had breast cancer, it was like a clock had started to tick. Surgery had removed the cancer, and I was beyond thankful, but I wanted my life back. There was this urgency to make up for lost time. It was as if I was standing still, yet watching my dreams recede from me—all while everyone else moved forward with their lives, leaving me behind.

Following the labyrinth's outer perimeter, I made my way at a pace that wasn't exactly meditative. Eventually, on a switchback, I came a stone's-width away from the center before the path veered away again, leading me with it. A wave of frustration spread through me. This was supposed to be an ancient form of wordless, meditative prayer! I nearly crossed the barrier of steppingstones to take a shortcut to the center—to get there faster.

But that would defeat the purpose, right? So, I made myself slow down and follow the path away, concentrating on letting my breath deepen. Once the winding path did finally open into the center, I read the engraved stone: "Stand at the crossroads and look; ask for the ancient paths, ask where the good way is, and walk in it, and you will find rest for your souls" (Jeremiah 6:16 NIV).

I realized God was telling me that he hasn't set me on a dead-end path. Although life is filled with switchbacks that seem to take me in the opposite direction of where I want to go, he is leading me toward the center—to him. I will get where I need to be if I just trust him with the path.

> *"I will get where I need to be if I just trust him with the path."*

PRAYER

Dear God, thank you for protecting us from the enemy's mazes, full of tricks and wrong turns, and instead, providing paths like the labyrinth's that always lead to the center, to you. Amen.

REFLECT

When have you felt like God wasn't leading you where you wanted to go, but it proved to be the best path for you?

chosen

GLORY

AND WE ALL, WITH UNVEILED FACE, BEHOLDING THE GLORY OF THE LORD, ARE BEING TRANSFORMED INTO THE SAME IMAGE FROM ONE DEGREE OF GLORY TO ANOTHER. FOR THIS COMES FROM THE LORD WHO IS THE SPIRIT.

2 CORINTHIANS 3:18 (ESV)

In the beginning, God made everything. He created a world full of his glorious beauty and power—a world he chose to share with us. With his words, God spoke the land, the sea, the sky into existence—and all living things—except humanity. We did not live until he breathed his own life into our lungs.

We became his children, made to walk with him and reflect his glorious presence. When we fell and could not save ourselves, his own Son stepped down from divine glory, humbling himself, and took on human form as our redeeming sacrifice. Jesus made it possible for God's Spirit to dwell in our hearts once again, transforming us into people through whom he can restore creation. His glory will come...on Earth as it is in Heaven. Will you be a place where his glory dwells?

A GIRL NAMED WHITNEY

"...It is for the glory of God, so that the Son of God may be glorified through it."

John 11:4 (ESV)

BY ABBIE LOVE

In August 1993, a scared 16-year-old walked into a hospital in Cebu, Philippines and soon gave birth to a healthy baby girl. Later that day, she snuck out, leaving the child she'd named Whitney, behind.

This is how my life began.

After my mother abandoned me, I lived in the hospital for three months, along with six other abandoned children. Out of fear that we would be handed over to the government and become lost orphans, the nurses hid us in a closet during the week and took us home with them on the weekends. They searched the city for our parents but never found them.

After three months, a children's shelter discovered what was happening at the hospital and was able to enter us into the system properly. When I was 14 months old, I was adopted by the Pitner family and moved to Colorado. As I grew up, I wrestled with why my birth mother abandoned me, and I couldn't understand how a loving God would let it happen.

When I turned 16, the same age that my birth mother was when she had me, I found myself looking for answers to questions I was scared to admit to anyone, including myself. How could someone abandon their own child? What did I do to deserve to be left behind? What part of me did she not want to be associated with?

Eventually, I gave my life to Jesus and embarked on a healing journey. I realized it no longer mattered why my mother abandoned me. God was protecting me the entire time. It no longer mattered what could have happened if she kept me; I knew God had a plan all along.

Sometimes, we don't understand the ways God uses to bring us into a new life. Like in John 11, Lazarus is dying, and his sisters, Mary and Martha, beg Jesus to come quickly to save him. Jesus says the illness will not lead to death. "It is for the glory of God, so that the Son of God may be glorified through it" (John 11:4 ESV). Jesus waits a couple days to travel to Judea, to visit Lazarus. In that time, Lazarus dies.

Four days later, Jesus stands before his tomb and tells them to roll the stone away. Martha cautions against it, but Jesus says, "Did I not tell you that if you believed you would see the glory of God?" Right before he raises Lazarus from the dead, he looks up to Heaven and says, "Father, I thank you that you have heard me. I knew that you always hear me..." (John 11:41 ESV).

I know that verse to be true, especially as I snuggle my own sweet little girl, whom I named Whitney. In the darkest parts of my life—in the desperation, the anger, the hurt, and the pain—God heard me. He has always heard me. He gave me a new life.

Nothing is too much for him. Every day, I look at my daughter and see the glory of God through her. I hope you, too, can find peace in the fact that there is nothing that we say or do that will turn God away from us, once we are his. He always has and always will hear us.

PRAYER

Father, thank you for never abandoning me. You know every detail of my life and yet, you still love and protect me. Help me to trust your plans even when I don't have the answers. Let me hear your voice as you hear mine. In Jesus' name, amen.

REFLECT

How have you seen God breathe new life into an area you thought was dead?

chosen

NO LONGER BOUND

My mouth will tell of your righteous deeds, of your saving acts all day long—though I know not how to relate them all. I will come and proclaim your mighty acts, Sovereign Lord; I will proclaim your righteous deeds, yours alone.

Psalm 71:15-16 (NIV)

BY PEYTON PICKENS

The first time I heard my dad share his testimony, I was so proud of how far he'd come. He'd gone from incarceration and drug addiction to completely sold out for Christ. There was one thing, however, my 8-year-old brain just couldn't comprehend. How was my dad able to talk about the most painful and traumatizing moments in his life with so much self-assurance?

As someone who grew up in church, I knew John 8:36 (NIV): "So if the Son sets you free, you will be free indeed!" I had recited and sung that scripture many times and genuinely believed I was free. But I carried a secret that held me captive in shame, guilt, and condemnation. It was a secret I kept from everyone in my life.

When I was 18 years old, I became pregnant by my boyfriend. Due to fear, ignorance, and pressure, I chose to have an abortion. I was so ashamed and traumatized by my decision, that I promised myself to take that secret to my grave. I didn't know how to cope, so I pushed myself into a state of denial. For 10 years, I pretended the abortion never happened.

When I attended my first Chosen Conference, I heard Pastor Irene Rollins teach about reframing your shame, and I listened in awe as she fearlessly shared her journey of overcoming alcoholism.

When she encouraged women struggling with shame and guilt to come forward to receive prayer, I found myself on my knees, sobbing in front of two women on the prayer team, confessing to the abortion.

The prayer I received that night was the beginning of my healing journey. Two days after the conference, I signed up for the Forgiven and Set Free abortion recovery small group. It was only after meeting with that small group and receiving healing I didn't even know I needed, that I was able to say, for the first time, "I am FREE!" I accepted God's forgiveness and became a new creation.

A year later, as I stood off to the side of the stage at a Sisterhood event, preparing to share my abortion testimony publicly for the first time in front of 300 women, I was hit with the answer to the question that 8-year-old me couldn't understand. It wasn't confidence that I had seen when my dad shared his testimony; it was the truth of Revelation 12:11. We will overcome Satan by the blood of the lamb and the word of our testimony. It wasn't self-assurance that empowered my dad or Pastor Irene to vulnerably share about the hard moments in their lives; it was freedom in Christ!

The Lord redeems us, enabling us to share our stories for his glory. He broke the chains of shame and guilt that the enemy kept me bound with for so long. Now, I can boldly proclaim the glory of God because he set this captive free!

> *"The prayer I received that night was the beginning of my healing journey."*

PRAYER

God, thank you for making a way for my freedom. By the blood of your Son, Jesus, I am free of guilt and shame and can move forward healed and restored. God, help me to be bold in how I share my testimony with others so they, too, can experience the life-giving freedom that you provide. To you be all the glory. In Jesus' name, amen.

REFLECT

How has the Lord worked through some of the toughest moments in your life?

chosen

LET THERE BE LIGHT

I WILL NOT KEEP SILENT BECAUSE OF ZION, AND I WILL NOT KEEP STILL BECAUSE OF JERUSALEM, UNTIL HER RIGHTEOUSNESS SHINES LIKE A BRIGHT LIGHT AND HER SALVATION, LIKE A FLAMING TORCH.

ISAIAH 62:1(CSB)

The Earth began formless and empty, with darkness covering the face of the deep. So, God created light to separate the darkness and called it good. He created the greater light of day and the lesser light of night to illuminate our world. And soon afterward, he made us in his image, to bear his light.

He gave us everything but still we wanted more. We forgot we were his image-bearers and moved along our own paths. Our light grew dim, and we became more comfortable in the shadows. But then, God sent his light into the world in the form of his only Son, to save us, to illuminate the path back to him.

Jesus stands as a beacon on the hill, drawing us to him. He comes not as a flicker, but as a flaming torch for everyone to see—to recognize him for who he truly is: our Savior, the Light of the World.

He reminds us of who we are—his image-bearers. We have the power of his light within us. He hands us the torch to stand on the surrounding hillsides in his name, to hold high his beacon of hope. We are to see it spread from one hill to another, until his light dispels the darkness and illuminates the entire earth.

Day 29

OUT OF THE DARKNESS AND INTO HIS LIGHT

In him was life, and that life was the light of all mankind.
The light shines in the darkness, and the darkness has not overcome it.

John 1:4-5 (NIV)

BY TIFFIN LAMOREAUX

As a child, I remember skinning my knee and hiding it from my mother, knowing she would want to clean the wound. To act like nothing had happened seemed a better, less painful option. I wasn't thinking about germs and debris getting caught under the skin. I just knew that cleaning the wound was going to hurt...badly, and I wanted to avoid that. So, I hid it, and it became infected.

Physical wounds aren't the only wounds that worsen if hidden or ignored. In my sophomore year of college, I was raped, and my virginity stolen by someone I didn't know. The person hid when a friend unexpectedly knocked on my door. Once my friend sensed something was wrong, she called campus security.

After being subjected to a sexual assault exam in the emergency department, I was told by one of the police officers who took my statement that it would be hard to prove that I had not consented. He said pressing charges would only bring disgrace to me and to my family, so I kept silent.

I allowed the trauma inflicted upon me to strip me of my worth, and those feelings of worthlessness led to sexual promiscuity, substance use, and other reckless behaviors—which left me feeling even more worthless. To combat those feelings, I sought perfection through performance: *If I perform well, nobody will see the darkness hiding inside.*

Over the years, it became harder to hide the darkest parts of my past inside my heart. After I married, I started to have panic attacks during intimate moments with my husband. My brain didn't register that the danger was over. Desperate, I turned to God, knowing I could not do this on my own. I needed his strength and his light to clear away the darkness.

Exposing our darkest sins and wounds to the light requires a level of vulnerability that can feel overwhelming and painful. In the same way that our physical wounds must be exposed, cleaned, and bandaged to heal—our mental, emotional, and spiritual wounds must also go through that same healing process. Only then, can the Light of Christ clean, bind, and heal them.

Slowly, I exposed the darkness to God, my counselor, and my husband. I underwent EMDR therapy, where traumatic memories are accessed in ways to help reprocess memories from the event to repair the mental wound. My counselor helped me reprocess my identity from worthless to worthy daughter of the King.

God, the ultimate physician, sent Jesus to be the Light of the World and heal us from sin. "The light shines in the darkness, and the darkness has not overcome it" (John 1:5 NIV). Let him speak truth, life, and light into the darkest areas of your life. Nothing in your past is too big for God to redeem.

> *"Let him speak truth, life, and light into the darkest areas of your life."*

PRAYER

Jesus, you are the Light that shines in the darkness. Thank you for enduring the cross so that our sins may be forgiven. You are the Great Physician. There is no wound you can't heal and no story you can't redeem. In Jesus' name, amen.

REFLECT

What hidden sins or wounds do you need to expose? What next step can you take to begin the healing process so God's light can shine through you?

chosen

LIGHT IN THE DARKNESS

When Jesus spoke again to the people, he said, "I am the light of the world. Whoever follows me will never walk in darkness, but will have the light of life."

John 8:12 (NIV)

BY KEENAN SCHRIVER

Have you ever felt like the light was slowly being extinguished from your life? Or maybe it didn't happen slowly at all. For me, within the span of six years, my mother-in-law passed away from cancer, my husband and I lost two babies early in pregnancy, my dad passed away from Covid, and my older brother died unexpectedly. Grief overwhelmed me in a way I wasn't sure would ever lift.

The darkness might have swallowed me, except that God never left me. He offered little glimpses of hope through people who encouraged me when I couldn't articulate what I needed. He showed me the beauty in his creation, in the sun and flowers. Although it was hard to read my Bible, to sing worship songs, or even formulate the words to pray, I had the foundation of my faith to protect that flicker of light and not let it go out.

John 8 tells us when we embrace Christ as Lord, we will no longer walk in darkness but in the light of the Lord. Even when our circumstances seem hopeless, his divine light is always in us. The light of Christ is a constant, life-giving presence that transforms everything. His light helped me to get out of bed to take care of my kids, to make it through some days without anxiety and panic, and more than anything, helped keep me going. Despite the darkness of my circumstances, I felt God's presence—closer, actually, than I had ever experienced.

To follow Christ doesn't mean we pretend the darkness isn't real—I'm sure we all have a testimony about how real the darkness is—but instead, we get to trust in the presence of his light in the darkest places. He fills us with a light that cannot fade, and that light helps us see past our immediate struggles and gives us the strength to endure.

For so long, I saw only a flicker of his light—maybe what I could handle at the time. But step by step, he led me to a place of deeper intimacy with him. As he guided me through the darkness, I realized that God's light was never a flicker, but a wildfire.

PRAYER

Dear God, thank you for Jesus—the Light of the World. Thank you for illuminating your light in the darkness. Thank you for guiding us, no matter our circumstances. Please help us to always look to the light. In the mighty and holy name of Jesus, amen.

REFLECT

Identify a time in your life that you experienced pain or suffering but also sensed Jesus' presence as the Light of The World.

chosen

"As he guided me through the darkness, I realized that God's light was never a flicker, but a wildfire."

KEENAN SCHRIVER

Now to him who is able to do immeasurably more than all we ask or imagine, according to his power that is at work within us, to him be glory in the church and in Christ Jesus throughout all generations, for ever and ever! Amen.

EPHESIANS 3:20–21 (NIV)

ACKNOWLEDGMENTS

We would like to thank all the brave women who have shared their stories in this devotional and in our Sisterhood magazines over the years. God has revealed his power in your lives, and we are honored that you chose vulnerability over fear to help other women find hope and healing. Thank you.

We also want to recognize our designers for their beautiful artwork and our proofreaders whose eagle eyes review all the details.

This book wouldn't exist without a conference, so we'd like to thank the women who walk through the doors of the Chosen Women's Conference every year, and to those who will in the future.

We have incredible teams at Seacoast Church who work tirelessly behind the scenes to create an experience at Chosen that we couldn't have dreamed of all those years ago. God has truly gifted them with unique talents and skills, and we are so grateful for all the ways they share them with us.

And most of all to you, our readers, thank you. It is our hope that God spoke to you through these pages. We hope that you now realize that God, your Creator, places great value on you. You are chosen. We pray that you use your own story to help others find freedom and purpose in their faith.

WAYS TO CONNECT

Discover a Community to Encourage You

SEACOAST CHURCH

Seacoast Church is a place where everyone is welcome, no matter where they are on their spiritual journey. Our mission is to help people find God, grow their faith, discover their purpose, and make a difference. Join us for weekly services at a location near you or online.

seacoast.org, IG seacoastchurch, facebook.com/seacoast
youtube.com/@SeacoastChurch

SEACOAST CHURCH

SEACOAST SISTERHOOD

Seacoast Sisterhood is a gathering of women from every season of life who desire to strengthen their faith within authentic community. Our prayer is that we will come together to comprehend the Word of God with our heads, be convicted in our hearts, and carry it out with our hands. Find a Sisterhood group or event at a location near you.

"And these God-chosen lives all around—what splendid friends they make!" (Psalm 16:3 MSG)

May God bless you with authentic friendships as you wholeheartedly seek him!

seacoast.org/women

SEACOAST SISTERHOOD